Positive Thinking

A Super Simple Guide to Stop Negativity, Transform your Life and Achieve Happiness

by Emma Jones

© 2016 Emma Jones
All Rights Reserved

Table of Contents

Positive Thinking

Table of Contents

Introduction

Chapter 1 – The Biology of Positive Thoughts

Chapter 2 – Negativity Effect/Bias

Chapter 3 – Replacing Negative with Positive

Chapter 4 – Simple Behavioral Therapy

Conclusion

Disclaimer

While all attempts have been made to verify the information provided in this book, the author does not assume any responsibility for errors, omissions, or contrary interpretations of the subject matter contained within. The information provided in this book is for educational and entertainment purposes only. The reader is responsible for his or her own actions and the author does not accept any responsibilities for any liabilities or damages, real or perceived, resulting from the use of this information.

Introduction

Most of the time we go through our day coping and dealing with issues as they arise. As we cope and deal we are making decisions, scrutinizing alternatives, summarizing and condensing, and hopefully focusing on our jobs and free time equally; at least that is what we hope we are doing.

In reality, many of us feel there isn't enough time in a day to accomplish all of these things, and we are not in control or focusing efficiently because we are stressed!

There are people who seem to move through their day unperturbed by the hectic commotion of work, life, and family. They are always chipper, ready with a sincere smile, and genuinely "happy".

These people rarely complain, always have time for a relaxing lunch, and seem to finish everything they start. Everyone knows people like this, and some of us might even find them annoying!

Ok, no more exclamation points, it is time to take control, reduce the stress, and think ourselves happy.

This is possible because psychology and biology/neuro-biology, say so. For instance, endorphins, oxytocin, epinephrine/adrenaline, dopamine, serotonin and encephalin, are a few naturally produced hormones/chemicals/neurotransmitters that are triggered by behavior, thoughts, and emotions. These biologically produced compounds can make us feel happy, anxious, frightened, threatened, angry, sleepy…the list goes on.

The truth is when we behave or think a certain way, our mind and body "unconsciously" responds by producing compounds that trigger emotions, that trigger thoughts, that can trigger behavior…it is in essence the circle of life.

Those happy people seem to have insight into this circle and how it works. Many of these "happy" people do yoga or engage in an esoteric practice of some sort…not really, but they are essentially happy and have lower stress levels.

You won't find any esoteric information in this book, but you will learn how to partake of those wonderful chemicals our body distributes for free, if we know how to ask.

The information in this book is simple, graceful, and effective, there are no important steps that must be performed properly or scientific jargon you need a PhD to understand.

Simple – the mind and body communicate without our conscious knowledge but we can intervene consciously whenever we choose.

Graceful – there is no secret or mystery to unravel, our subconscious is real and it is our autonomic nervous system.

Effective – we can consciously think and behave in ways that will diminish negativity, support positivity, and help us achieve happiness.

In this book, you will also learn how to replace negative thoughts and behaviors with positive ones. It is amazing how easy it is to achieve happiness and maintain it when you learn to focus on positive thoughts and release negative ones.

Learning to be an optimist is not difficult when you realize it can mentally change your life.

CBT is covered in the last chapter, CBT, or cognitive behavioral therapy is a good way to get in touch with yourself and the reasons you think the way you do. Positive thinking works best when it is anchored in real facts and CBT will help you uncover the best way for you to achieve permanent happiness.

This journey to happiness will go a lot smoother when you understand yourself on a deeper level.

Before you begin reading and changing your life for the better, get yourself a nice journal. Find one that makes you feel good when you open it and write in it.

 Get yourself a nice pen too, if you enjoy using the pen and the journal they will work even better for you!

You will need this journal and pen to record all the wonderful, positive thoughts you are about to think…and you will need them to eliminate any lingering negativity that tries to stick around.

Positive thinking works on paper as well as in your head. Writing down your thoughts, emotions, and understanding will help you achieve exactly what you are striving for. It is always helpful to read over your thoughts and insights from beginning to end. It can be uplifting to see how far you have come and how much you have achieved.

Chapter 1 – The Biology of Positive Thoughts

If you fill your mind with negative thoughts, your brain will naturally make lots of negative connections; if you change your thoughts to positive, your brain will naturally make lots of positive connections.

Neurons, neural pathways and synapses form and work according to the data received; if you are filling your mind with negative data, the brain will help you stay on track, and negative.

It's true, our brains eliminate or create connections based on learning and repetition.

From the moment, we are born, our brains begin to make connections, learn, grow, and change.

This ability to learn, grow, and change never disappears, you can learn, grow, and change until the day you die. We know that our ability to learn depends on repetition.

Think about it, when you bought your first smart phone, you learned to use it through repetition. Our brains love repetition.

There is no reason to explain exactly how the brain uses repetition to learn, grow, and change; all we need to know is that the more we repeat something, the more the brain learns.

From a biological standpoint, the brain functions best when we repeat our actions and thoughts. The brains ability to learn and form new connections and remove old ones is called neuroplasticity.

Lucky for us, neuroplasticity ensures that we can change our thought patterns, beliefs and behaviors by "thinking".

Our minds respond to outside influences and learn by making connections subconsciously as well as consciously. It is important to consciously "think" about information we gather, thinking about the information gives us a chance support positive connections.

When negative statements and thoughts are repeated over and over, the subconscious begins to accept them as fact and the autonomous nervous system is triggered.

This is why we never forget how to ride a bike, write our name, dial our phone number…these things are repeated so much, it is second nature. The same thing is true for negative thoughts and associations.

Positive thoughts have the same effect on the brain when they are repeated over and over. Always use positive, supportive, and loving words to describe yourself, your brain will favor those affirmations over negative ones because they are repeated. It sounds too simple to be true, but it is.

As children, we learn to navigate our social and physical world by watching our parents and through direct experience. Although we learn through direct experience, these experiences are filtered through what we have learned from our parents.

Not everyone has had the same upbringing or the same experiences, repeated negativity or positive reinforcement through direct experience and parental involvement provides us with the information we use to develop a core belief.

When we were children we did not "rationalize" our experiences, we just incorporated them into our learning process and moved on. As adults, we have the ability to rationalize our experiences and take from them what we want and leave out what we don't want.

Even though we now can think and rationalize, we still fall back on experience gained in childhood because our brain was in hyper drive, it soaked up everything and made an enormous amount of neural connections.

It is important to understand that the brain gathers information from all of our senses, all of our interactions, and all of our activities, and we have the ability to filter that information by thinking and reflecting on our thoughts.

Reflecting on the reasons behind our negative thoughts and behaviors can and does change the information we keep and the information we discard.

The more positive association you create, the more your brain will focus on those positive qualities around you and inside you. Positive associations can be just as strong as negative associations.

Our brains may focus on negative associations quicker than positive ones, but if we build positive associations and block negative ones, we can change the biology of our brain.

How to Build Positive Associations

- Make an effort to remain aware of your surroundings and note the positive aspects of your environment and the people in it

- Be in the moment and take the time to look for something uplifting in those around you and in the environment

- Comment on positive qualities you see in others

- Exercise because it releases stress reducing chemicals in the brain, think about how exercising is important for your health and how it makes you feel

You will experience changes in your thoughts and feelings almost immediately when you begin to build positive brain associations.

When you behave in a positive way, others will too, and this will strengthen positive associations.

Practice smiling, this may seem silly, but if you actively practice smiling, you will receive positive reinforcement from others because most of them will smile back.

Simple Tips to Remember

- The brain can learn, grow, and change until the day you die
- Reflect on the reasons for your negative thoughts
- Repeat positive associations and thoughts

- Keep your focus on the present

The Power of Positive Thinking on Physical Health

Doctors know that positive thinking makes a big impact on pain thresholds, recovery time, and healing.

When a person has, a positive outlook going into surgery, their recovery is quicker than those who lack a positive attitude.

Interestingly, optimists have stronger immune systems and get sick less frequently than those with a pessimistic attitude.

There are also specific biological changes that take place when someone experiences positive emotions and the same is true for those who experience negative or traumatic emotions.

The pain of a broken heart can actually manifest as physical pain in the chest; blood vessels constrict, and in some cases, it has been noted that arrhythmias can develop.

In sharp contrast to the physical symptoms experienced when an individual is suffering from a broken heart, those who experience love receive an extra opioid boost produced by the body.

Hugging, kissing, and loving physical contact trigger the release of oxytocin, and as the name suggests, oxytocin is a natural opioid produced by the body.

Infants and mothers experience a release of oxytocin when they are in physical contact with each other. This release of oxytocin helps to cement the bond between them. Mothers release oxytocin when they breast feed, and this release of oxytocin relaxes both mother and child. Oxytocin is a reward that conditions the brain to repeat the activity that triggered the release.

When feel good chemicals are released into our blood stream we experience pleasure, and this pleasure ensures we will repeat the actions that triggered the release.

Positive thoughts also trigger the release of feel good chemicals. The interplay between positive thoughts and emotions and the body's own behavioral conditioning.

Infants in NICU thrive better when the mother is allowed to hold the baby and caress the baby. The physical touch of the mother calms the infant and reduces stress for both mother and child.

The subtle but obvious advantages gained physically and mentally by a mother and her baby in the NICU shows the power of positive behavior and thought.

Another interesting correlation exists between positive thoughts and health that Doctors have recognized.

Praying for sick patients speeds recovery, regardless of religion, the improvement is real. Prayer is positive thinking, and the effects it has on patients is proof that it works.

Laughter is a positive emotion and behavior that speeds recovery. Laughter can lower blood pressure, reduce pain, and lower stress. The old adage "laughter is the best medicine" is actually true.

Chapter 2 – Negativity Effect/Bias

Humans are predisposed to focus on negativity when a situation can be either positive or negative.

Basically, survival of the fittest has helped us make the leap from Ape to Human, and we have inherited some pretty impressive abilities from this evolutionary journey.

One of these abilities is to make assumptions based on stereotyping, and both of these abilities focus more on negative attributes rather than positive ones.

Now before this gets out of hand, stereotyping is something that has served us well in the past.

We like to organize everything into neat little packages that can be stored away and pulled out when we need them. Humans are creatures of habit, and habitually organizing has helped us as we struggled along the road from monkey to human.

Our brains love organization, organization helps us remember, and remembering helps us do just about everything.

The problem with stereotyping becomes obvious when we make assumptions, like judging a book by its cover.

Evolution however, has decided that stereotyping and assuming is an important component of survival…and focusing on the potential negativity has always been the "safe" bet; this leaves us modern humans with a dilemma when we are faced with a person, place, or thing, we are unfamiliar with.

If we have no real-life experience with this person, place, or thing, we are apt to liken it to something we have experience with…so we stereotype and assume.

Assumptions and stereotyping are perceived as negative behaviors to engage in, our modern sensibilities are bruised by these types of behaviors.

Although modern society does not condone stereotyping or assuming, our subconscious has no such problem with it.

It is socially unacceptable to stereotype and it is just as bad to assume; but the truth is, people do it everyday and the subconscious reacts to it.

Negativity Effect or Negativity Bias really is stereotyping and assuming with a new label.

When an individual makes negative assumptions about a person, place, or thing, or when an individual relies on negative stereotyping for information about a person, place, or thing, they are caught up in the Negativity Effect/Bias.

Examples of the Negativity Effect or Negativity Bias

- Person/People/Groups: "My ex-husband cheated on me and lied about it" Men *are cheats and liars*

- Place/Situation: "My friend vacationed in Hawaii, stayed in a hotel, and now her home is infested bedbugs!" *Hawaii is a dirty place to visit, they have lots of bedbugs there* or *I don't want to go on vacation, hotels have bedbugs*

- Objects/Things: "John used the printer in the copy room and it had a paper jam" Printers *are useless, paper always gets jammed in them*

These examples are simple but they show how negativity invades our thoughts through Negativity Effect/Bias.

If we were to individualize every person, place, and thing we come across in our lifetimes we would not be able to process all of the information coming in.

So, are we doomed to rely on negative stereotypes and negative assumptions? No, absolutely not, we can rely on positive thoughts and behaviors to help us get rid of negativity.

Simple Tips to Remember

- The brain favors negative when given a choice

- Don't give the brain a choice focus on positive over negative

- Think about and rationalize negative stereotypes or assumptions you have

Chapter 3 – Replacing Negative with Positive

The simple conscious act of recognizing negative thoughts is where this journey to happy begins. Many of us repeat negative statements in our heads or even engage in complaint filled conversations.

If you were to make a note of it every time you thought something negative, or made a negative comment, or engaged in a negative conversation, you would be able to fill a notebook a day.

Noticing negative thoughts when they occur is one way to begin taking control of your happiness. Each time a negative thought comes to mind, tweak it…give it a positive spin or engage in a positive behavior.

You will get better and better at this the more you practice. Your goal is to notice as many negative thoughts as you can and make them positive.

Each time you replace a negative thought with a positive behavior or thought you are sending a signal to your subconscious.

The more you do this, the quicker your subconscious will begin to focus on the positive thoughts.

You are building a bridge between your conscious and autonomic nervous system.

How to Stop a Negative Thought

- When the thought occurs say the word stop in your head. Disrupt the thought as soon as it surfaces, breaking the chain of thought with the word stop will help you keep negativity at bay.

- Rationalize the negative thought when it surfaces, *why do you think this? What triggered the thought in the first place?*

- Write it down, get a journal and write down your negative thoughts. Read through your journal and rationalize the thoughts and behaviors. Break down negative assumptions and write down any new positive understandings you have realized.

Replacing a negative thought before it becomes a negative behavior is the best outcome. When a negative thought arises, it can trigger a negative behavior, for instance; you know you have to speak in front of your colleague's tomorrow, you tell yourself, "I hate speaking in front of crowds, I am so awkward."

Telling yourself you don't like to speak in front of crowds because you are awkward is not a true statement.

You may feel awkward, but you are not awkward, you wouldn't have a job where you have to speak to a crowd if you were truly awkward.

Be truthful and construct a new thought, "speaking in front of crowds makes me feel awkward" is not as discouraging as the first thought.

The more you recognize and catch those negative thoughts, the more adept you will become at replacing them with positive, encouraging thoughts and statements.

Write down those negative thoughts and when you have time, read through them and re-write them in a more accurate and truthful way.

You will be pleasantly surprised how quickly this exercise begins to change your thought patterns.

When we are stressed, it seems like blowing off steam is the best way to feel better. The truth is, if you are blowing off steam by complaining and exaggerating the situation, you are only adding to the negativity. The best way to "blow off steam" is to go and do something you enjoy, do something positive.

You can replace the negativity of the day with positive thoughts and emotions by engaging in an activity that you enjoy.

Ranting about negative things that happened during the day won't help you feel better…doing something you enjoy will replace the negative with a positive…end your day on a happy note.

Positive affirmations and a positive self-image play an important part in achieving happiness. The cliché, "if you don't love yourself, you can't love someone else" is true.

If you have a poor self-image, the positive emotions that bond a people together are not readily available. Positive affirmations will only get you so far, you need both to achieve happiness.

Positive affirmations are uplifting, supportive, statements that will help you attain a positive self-image.

Achieving and maintaining a positive self-image requires self-respect and self-love. Write down 5 of your best qualities, then read them off to yourself. Keep these 5 qualities in the forefront of your mind and call on them when you are feeling bad about yourself.

The easiest way to find some positive affirmations is to look them up on the internet. There are millions of quotes available online, spend some time researching positive affirmations and quotes, then write down your favorites and keep them in your journal.

These affirmations are a way for you to express how you feel about yourself.

Whenever stress gets you down, or you are having a bad day, spend a few minutes reading through your positive affirmations, they will help you fight the negativity. Never be to harsh or beat yourself up when things don't go as planned.

Remember, you only want what's best for yourself, you are not the enemy.

The more time you spend focusing on positive thoughts and feelings, the less time you have to pay attention to negativity.

Bad things happen, things don't always go your way, but, these things only have power over your life if you give them that power.

It's ok to acknowledge mistakes, it is not ok to call them failures. Mistakes can motivate you to new heights of achievement instead of dragging you under and drowning you in failure.

Simple Tips to Remember

- Stop negative thoughts the moment they rise to the surface…Stop!

- Rationalize your negative thoughts, talk to yourself…ask yourself why?

- Write down your negative thoughts and feelings in a journal

- Replace negative thoughts with positive behaviors, engage in something you enjoy

The more you actively work to change negative to positive, the more receptive your subconscious will become to positive associations and assumptions.

Negativity is subjective, your perception of situations, people, and things will change if you stop those thoughts and question them when they occur. Don't exaggerate negative perceptions of yourself, and be truthful with yourself.

Always accept responsibility for your actions, positive thinking is only effective if you are honest with yourself.

It can be difficult to identify negative thoughts and replace them with positive ones if you don't recognize your own responsibility.

Take the time to think your behavior through, and if you are to blame, accept it and move on. Denial only leads to more negative thoughts and actions, own it and let it go.

Chapter 4 – Simple Behavioral Therapy

Behavioral therapy can be a simple and effective way to implement positive thinking and help you achieve happiness.

Behavioral therapy works on the premise that negative associations can be replaced with positive associations through repetitive behavior. Our brains are always making associations, it is how the brain learns.

Using cognitive behavioral therapy to reinforce positive thinking and achieve happiness can be accomplished with a little bit of practice.

Therapists and those who work in the field of psychology use CBT, cognitive behavioral therapy, to help people work through psychological problems; and it is a great way to rid yourself of negativity.

CBT is effective and easy to incorporate into your own positive thinking journey. Learning why you behave and think the way you do makes it easier for you to identify negativity and let it go.

These techniques are simplified for the purpose of positive thinking, you are not working through any psychological issues, you just want to support positive thoughts and eliminate the negative.

Simple CBT to Encourage Positive Thinking

- Refocusing
- Mindfulness
- Core Beliefs
- CBT Worksheet

Refocusing

Refocusing is a simple technique for practicing positive thinking. Most of the time, negative thoughts demand more focus than positive ones, this is why refocusing can help.

Every time your mind begins to focus on negativity, you must make a conscious effort to redirect the mind by stopping the thought, then focus on a positive association.

Here is an example of how to refocus:

You have an argument with your best friend

Negative thought – "she always gets angry over such stupid things"

Emotion – anger and blame

Result – you don't apologize or attempt to repair the relationship and you lose a good friend

Refocus

Positive thought – "I didn't have to get so angry, we are both stubborn, I should apologize"

Emotion – remorseful and forgiving

Result – your apology opens the lines of communication and the two of you resolve your differences

When you refocus you make an honest attempt to understand both sides of an issue. Conceptualizing both scenarios gives you a clear understanding of the results negativity can cause and how a positive refocus can change the outcome for the better.

It is not always easy to see both sides, but this exercise will strengthen your ability to refocus.

No matter what issue you are dealing with, rationalize both sides, the negative and the positive then refocus your thoughts.

You will have to do this several times before you begin to rationalize both sides automatically.

The point is to frame your understanding and provide a potential outcome scenario for both sides, this helps to change the way you think.

Mindfulness

Mindfulness is the ability to be present in the moment and aware of your surroundings. Mindfulness reduces negativity because it helps you to focus on the environment and the people around you.

Notice that others react to you and your behavior, understand that others may not be mindful.

Practice taking in your surroundings and make your space one you enjoy spending time in. If you work in an office be mindful of your work space, if you like plants, add one to your desk. If your chair is uncomfortable, try adjusting your posture. Take small breaks from your work and stretch, pay attention to you feel physically and mentally.

When you practice being mindful it is easier to stop negative thoughts when they rise to the surface.

It is easier to appreciate the small things and focus on positive thoughts when you are purposeful in your behavior.

Do not let your mind wander aimlessly, give your thoughts direction and practice being mindful of everything including your mood.

An Exercise in Mindfulness

Write down these three questions and answer them everyday for a week. This will help you recognize how mindfulness shapes your thoughts and behavior.

How many people have you smiled at today?

How many times did you laugh today?

Describe a pleasant conversation you had today?

Core Beliefs

Core beliefs are the result of experiences that form a filter through which you view the world around you.

Cultures have core beliefs, religions have core beliefs, and individuals have core beliefs. Your core beliefs shape your understanding of experiences. Negative core beliefs make it difficult to shake negative thoughts and emotions.

At first it may be difficult to narrow down your personal core beliefs. Once you identify them, you can modify them so they support positive thinking and help you achieve lifelong happiness.

Sometimes a simple core belief can color your entire perspective and make everyday life aggravating and ultimately miserable. The good news is you can change those beliefs, they are not carved in stone.

Here are a few examples of core beliefs and how they can block positive thinking:

1. Core belief – Success if for the strong

Negative block – failure means you are weak – each time you do not achieve your goal you are not just a failure, you are weak – others who fail are weak

2. Core belief – The world is an uncaring place

Negative block – distrust – people only care about themselves - if someone is kind they have ulterior motives

3. Core belief – Optimism is naïve

Negative block – hope is silly – reality is harsh – if someone is optimistic they are going to be taken advantage of

Identifying negative core beliefs and modifying them will allow you to process information in a more positive way. Think about your core beliefs and write them down and reflect on how they shape your view of the world.

Once you are familiar with your own core beliefs you can begin to modify them, you cannot just change them and make them positive, they must be modified through reflection in a thoughtful, mindful, and rational way.

An Exercise in Modifying Core Beliefs

Answer these questions for each core belief listed above. This exercise will help you understand how your own core beliefs influence your world view, and how you can work to modify them.

How can this core belief be understood in a different positive way?

Is there a truth or opposing point of view that challenges that statement?

How does this core belief hold me back?

There is no need to see a psychology professional for help with positive thinking. However, these simple techniques are helpful for understanding yourself and why you think the way you do.

It is much easier to make changes and think positive when you understand yourself and your motives.

There is no set amount of time you need to practice these techniques, just learning them and understanding them will probably be enough to help you along.

Conclusion

Positive thinking really can transform your life and help you achieve happiness. The happiest people are optimists and an optimist always thinks positive.

Optimism is more than a personality trait, it is a way of interacting with the world and anyone can become an optimist.

Do your best to actively and purposely live each day, and remember to keep a journal.

Once you achieve the happiness you desire, look back through your journal and you will be amazed how effective your efforts have been.

The information, tips, and exercises in this book will serve you well on your life journey.

Printed in Great Britain
by Amazon